BEFORE I MADE HISTORY™

LET'S SPLIT LOGS, ABE LINCOLN!

BY PETER AND CONNIE ROOP

SCHOLASTIC INC.

New York   Toronto   London   Auckland   Sydney
Mexico City   New Delhi   Hong Kong   Buenos Aires

For John — our favorite humorous storyteller,
compassionate lawyer, and steadfast friend
— P.R. and C.R.

ISBN 0-439-43926-4

10 9   9 10 11 12 13 14 15 16/0

Printed in the U.S.A.   40
First printing, January 2003

TABLE OF CONTENTS

INTRODUCTION

Abraham Lincoln had many nicknames during his life. Do you know he did not like being called Abe?

One of Abraham Lincoln's nicknames was "Honest Abe." Do you know how he got this nickname?

Young Abraham Lincoln lived in three states. Do you know which ones?

All of his life Abe Lincoln liked to learn. Do you know how many years Abe was actually in school?

Abe Lincoln liked to write, but his family was poor. Do you know what he wrote on instead of paper?

Abraham Lincoln had a hero whom he admired. Do you know who it was?

Abraham Lincoln ran in many elections. Do you know which one he was the most proud of?

President Lincoln was our tallest president. Do you know how tall he was?

President Lincoln was the first president to grow a beard. Do you know who asked him to grow it?

Abraham Lincoln died while he was President. Did you know he almost accidentally died twice when he was young?

The answers to these questions lie in who Abraham Lincoln was as a boy and as a young man.

This book is about Abraham Lincoln before he made history.

1
ABRAHAM LINCOLN IS BORN

On Sunday, February 12, 1809, the dawn was bright and cold. Winter winds blew around Tom and Nancy Lincoln's small Kentucky cabin. Frost sparkled and smoke rose from the chimney. Sunlight shone through the only window in the one-room log cabin.

Nancy smiled as she held her baby. Tom threw wood onto the fire and then he covered Nancy and the baby with a warm bearskin. Suddenly, the door opened. In dashed nine-year-old Dennis Hanks. Dennis was the baby's cousin. He yanked off his coonskin cap.

"What are you going to name him, Nancy?" he asked.

"Abraham, after his grandfather," Nancy answered. "Abraham Lincoln." Nancy handed Abraham to Dennis.

"Be careful, Dennis," Nancy said. "You are the first boy he's ever seen."

Dennis looked at the baby's red, wrinkled face. Abraham was crying and Dennis was afraid to hold his screaming cousin. He quickly handed him back.

"Take him!" Dennis said. "He'll never amount to much."

Dennis was wrong!

When Abe was born, Tom and Nancy Lincoln had lived on their Kentucky farm for three years. Sarah Lincoln, Abe's sister, had been born there in 1807. Sarah was two years old when Abe was born. Sarah was eager for her little brother to grow up so she would have someone to play with.

The Lincolns named their farm Sinking Spring Farm for the cool spring water bubbling out of a cave on the property. The spring was the best part of the farm.

The soil was thin and poor. Tom worked

hard to raise food for his family, but he never seemed to get ahead.

Tom hunted deer, bear, turkey, and squirrel for meat to eat. He liked making things out of wood and had made the cradle in which Nancy rocked Abe. He built the one-room log cabin in which Abe was born. He built the Lincolns' tables, chairs, stools, and beds. The Lincoln cabin was small. But for baby Abe, it was a cozy home.

While Tom worked outside, Nancy cared for Sarah and Abe inside. Nancy cooked the family's meals over a crackling wood fire. She washed and mended clothes and she spun wool and flax into thread to weave into cloth to make new clothes. Pioneer families like the Lincolns called flax and wool cloth "linsey-woolsey."

Nancy talked and sang to Sarah and Abe. She read the Bible to them and told them stories. She hugged them when they were sad or hurt. She laughed with them. Abe and Sarah loved their mother very much.

Soon, Abe was crawling on the dirt floor.

Then he stood, holding onto the chair and the table. Abe seemed to grow as fast and tall as a young tree. Nancy constantly made Abe new shirts because he outgrew them so quickly.

Young Abe was curious. He watched the world around him. He watched his father carry water from the spring and he saw Sarah help their mother make supper. He stared at his mother's spinning wheel going round and round and he gazed at the flames flickering in the fireplace. Abe watched and watched.

He didn't say much when he learned to talk. But he smiled and laughed. Abe learned to work early. He would carry a stick or two of wood to his mother for the fire. He dipped water from the spring into Sarah's water bucket. He wasn't strong enough to carry the bucket, but he kept Sarah company as she carried the heavy water bucket. Abe enjoyed his small world of the cabin, the farm, and the bubbling spring. But when Abe was two years old, that world changed.

2
ABE MOVES TO A NEW FARM

Tom Lincoln had grown restless. There were problems with Sinking Spring Farm. He wanted a better farm.

One day, the four Lincolns packed their belongings onto a wagon. They rolled eight miles to another farm that Tom had carved from the wilderness. Knob Creek ran through this farm, so they called it Knob Creek Farm.

Abe enjoyed Knob Creek. The Lincolns were very poor, but Abe had a good life. Most of the year he ran barefoot. In the winter, he wore moccasins. His pants were made of buckskin and he wore linsey-woolsey shirts. When it was cold, Abe wore a coonskin cap.

Abe played in the fields and the forest

with his sister, Sarah. She called him Abe even though he liked Abraham better. When Abe was two years old, he could hold a fishing pole and fish in Knob Creek. He followed bees to their hives. The sticky honey was the only sweet treat Abe had ever tasted.

As Abe got older, he worked harder. At age five, he carried armloads of wood for the cooking fire. He carried water and he fed the animals. Abe planted seeds with his father in their seven-acre field. He dug a hole, dropped in two seeds, and then covered the seeds with soil. Abe dug another hole, and another. The work was hard, but Abe loved to see the tiny green sprouts grow into tall plants.

One night, when Abe was seven years old, disaster struck. Abe and his father had planted corn and pumpkin seeds. That night lightning flashed and thunder crashed. Heavy rains washed away all the seeds. Abe and his father went back to work. They had to plant another crop of corn and pumpkins in order to survive.

Another time the Lincolns suffered a great sadness. Tom and Nancy had a new baby boy. They named him Thomas after his father. But young Thomas got sick and died. Tom Lincoln made a small casket and the Lincolns buried Thomas on their farm.

One day, seven-year-old Abe had a serious accident. Knob Creek was flooding. Abe was hunting with his friend Austin Gollaher. Abe saw some birds on the other side of the rushing creek and he wanted to get closer. He found a wet, slippery log bridging the creek. Abe carefully stepped on it. He took another step, then another. He had to be careful.

When Abe reached the middle of the stream, he slipped! He plunged into the raging stream and went underwater. Abe could not swim! Austin picked up a strong stick and held it out to his struggling friend. Abe grabbed the stick and Austin pulled him safely to shore. Abe and Austin decided not to tell their parents about Abe's accident.

They did not want to be punished for being so foolish.

The Lincoln farm was beside the Cumberland Trail. This busy road ran from Nashville, Tennessee, to Louisville, Kentucky. Abe liked to watch people on the trail. They were pioneer families — like the Lincolns — looking for new homes. Some families rolled by in covered wagons while others walked or rode horses. Abe met trappers and traders coming and going. He saw farmers riding to town for supplies. Whenever the travelers stopped, Abe listened to their stories and tales. He learned there was a wide world beyond the Kentucky hills and valleys.

One sunny day, Abe went fishing and caught a fine, fat fish. Abe hurried home to give the fish to his mother to cook for supper. Along the way, Abe met a soldier. The soldier was tired and hungry. Abe's parents believed in treating others nicely. Abe had been taught to share what food he had just as his parents shared their food when unexpected guests came to their cabin. Abe gave his fish to the soldier. The man was very grateful for young Abe's kindness. All his life Abe Lincoln would remember how pleased the soldier was with the kind gift of the fish.

One of Abe's favorite visitors often stopped at the Lincoln's cabin when he traveled along the Cumberland Trail. This visitor was named Christopher Columbus Graham. Mr. Graham was writing a book about the animals, trees, flowers, and rocks of the Kentucky wilderness. He'd open his knapsack and out would spill his treasures — strange rocks, odd old bones, unusual plants, and dried snakeskins. Abe enjoyed touching and learning about these natural wonders. When Mr. Graham visited the Lincolns, he told wonderful stories of hunting bears or being chased by enemies. Abe loved listening to Mr. Graham tell stories. One night, he told about camping with Daniel Boone. Abe listened eagerly. His grandfather — Abraham Lincoln, for whom he was named — had also been a friend of Daniel Boone's.

3

ABE LEARNS MANY LESSONS

Some things along the Cumberland Trail were not pleasant. One day, Abe saw slaves walking slowly along the dusty trail. The slaves were chained together and their master carried a long whip. Abe knew slavery was wrong. His parents were against slavery. Many farmers told Tom Lincoln he needed slaves to make his farm better, but Tom always said he would never own another person.

Abe learned a lot in the woods and fields, but he also wanted to learn to read and write. His father wanted Abe to be good with his hands not his mind. *What good was reading and writing when a man had to work hard on a farm to support a family?* he thought. So instead of going to school, Abe learned to do more jobs on the farm.

Abe's mother could read, but she could not write. She signed her name with an X. Nancy was determined that Abe and Sarah would learn how to read and write. Nancy told Tom it was time the children learned to read, write, and count. Tom agreed, but said that Abe and Sarah must do all of their chores, too.

Finally, Abe could go to school! He was six years old. Abe and Sarah walked two miles through the woods to Mr. Riney's log cabin school. Abe's dog, Honey, often went with them. Mr. Riney's school had one room with a fireplace to warm it. Like many poor children, Abe and Sarah paid Mr. Riney with firewood or food. Tom Lincoln had no money to spare for school learning.

In Mr. Riney's class, Abe learned his ABC's. He proudly printed his name with a feather pen. A-b-r-a-h-a-m L-i-n-c-o-l-n. He learned his numbers. The children at Abe's school were all different ages, from six to fourteen years old. Each student repeated his or her lessons out loud.

The school was very noisy. People called Abe's school a "blab school" for all of the blabbing that went on. Abe did not mind. He was glad to be in school, any school. He called his school the "ABC school."

After school, Abe did his chores. He cleaned the fireplace and brought in more wood. He plowed, planted, and weeded. Abe learned words out of a spelling book the Lincolns owned. He learned words with two letters, then three, and then four.

At night, Tom Lincoln told stories. Abe enjoyed his hunting adventures, but he was especially fond of the stories about his grandfather who fought in the Revolutionary War.

When he was alone, Abe told stories, too. Abe was shy and would not tell his stories to others. Instead, he told stories to himself as he plowed and when he rested. Once, after hearing a sermon, Abe stood on a stump and repeated the preacher's words out loud. Only the animals in the forest heard Abe Lincoln's speech.

When he was eight years old and could safely handle an ax, Abe split logs into firewood. His father taught Abe how to whittle pegs with a sharp knife and how to shape boards for building.

When the berries were ripe, Abe and Sarah picked blueberries, blackberries, and raspberries. Sarah helped her mother cook the delicious berries and preserve them for winter. Abe spread the rest of the berries out in the sun to dry.

Abe found time to play. He roamed the woods. Once, his father bought him a toy wagon for eight and one-third cents. Abe must have loved the toy because pioneer children had few toys to play with.

On hot summer days, Abe swam with his friend Austin Gollaher. After his fall into the creek, Abe wanted to be able to swim in case he had any more accidents like that.

One day, when he was seven years old,

Abe and Austin wanted to climb a tree. The boys took off their coonskin caps and set them on the ground. Abe climbed first. When he looked down at the caps, Abe decided to trick Austin. He would drop a juicy, ripe pawpaw fruit into Austin's cap. Austin saw what Abe was up to and switched the caps.

Abe dropped the pawpaw and it smashed into the cap. Austin laughed. Suddenly, Abe understood what happened. His own cap was filled with the juicy pawpaw! Abe laughed, too — the joke was on him!

Sometimes, Abe would stop what he was doing and just daydream. Big thoughts swirled around in young Abe Lincoln's head. But Abe kept these thoughts to himself, for he was just a poor boy growing up on a wilderness farm.

4

A NEW HOME IN INDIANA

One day, Tom Lincoln told his family they were moving again. Knob Creek Farm was no good. No matter how hard they worked, they could not make a living there. Tom needed more help, but he refused to own slaves. So they had to move to a new farm in Indiana because the soil was rich. Plus, Indiana did not allow slavery.

Abe helped his father build a raft. Tom loaded his tools and some trade goods onto the rough raft. He waved good-bye to his family as the raft drifted down Knob Creek into the Scott River and then on to the wide Ohio River. When Tom found a good farm, he would return for his family.

While Tom was gone, Abe was the man on

the farm. He did all of his father's farm jobs. There was no time for school.

Finally, Abe's father came home. He had claimed one hundred sixty acres of land near Pigeon Creek, Indiana. Tom told his family about the black soil, deer, turkeys, and bears. He did not tell Sarah and Abe that they would have to carry water from a distant spring.

The Lincolns packed. Nancy shook the corn shucks out of their mattresses and folded the coverings. Her few pots, pans, knives, and spoons were packed. The family Bible and spelling book were wrapped in a sack. Abe and Sarah had nothing to take except their spare clothes. Everything the Lincolns owned was loaded onto two horses. They left their furniture behind. Tom would make new furniture when they reached Indiana.

Carrying his father's gun, Abe walked in front as they began their journey to a new home in a new state. The year was 1816, and Abe was seven years old. If the Lincolns could travel in a straight line, the new farm on Pigeon Creek was only fifty miles away. But they couldn't. There were hills to climb and streams to cross. Two tiring days later, they reached the banks of the Ohio River. Abe had never seen a river so wide. The Lincolns crossed the Ohio on a ferryboat. Tom and Abe cut a trail through the woods.

Finally, they reached the brush piles Tom had made to claim his farm. Tom had not yet built a cabin. Winter was coming, so Tom and Abe quickly built a simple wooden shelter. Three sides were covered with bark and the fourth side was open. Tom and Abe built a fireplace. The half-faced shelter was cold when the rain and snow blew in. Day and night they fed wood into the fire to warm the hut and keep dangerous animals away. Abe cut more wood. Swinging the heavy ax kept him warm, and burning the wood kept everyone warm.

Hunting was good. Tom shot deer and bears. The furry hides were welcomed in the chilly open shelter. Sarah and Abe hiked a mile to get water from the spring.

As the long winter ended, Tom and Abe cleared the land for farming. They hitched a plow to a horse and Tom guided the horse as the plow cut through the earth. Abe followed, planting corn seeds as he had been doing since he was little.

When the crops were planted, Abe and his father built their new log cabin. It had one room. Mud and straw were packed in the cracks. The roof was made from shingles that Abe had split with his ax. There was a fireplace at one end and a table in the middle. The floor was dirt. Tom didn't make a wooden door but hung a bearskin instead. There was no window.

Abe's parents and Sarah slept at one end of the cabin. Abe slept in the attic loft that he and his father built. Each night, Abe climbed wooden pegs up to his mattress. When it rained, water dripped on Abe. The cold wind whistled through the cracks. Stars twinkled and the moon shone through the same cracks. This was to be Abe's home for the next thirteen years.

5
ABE'S LIFE CHANGES

Abe grew strong swinging his ax, carrying wood and water, and doing his chores. All his life, Abe Lincoln worked hard. He did not enjoy hard work, but he did his fair share so the Lincolns could survive. Abe once said his father taught him how to work hard, but he didn't teach him to love it.

Most pioneer boys were skilled hunters and they provided meat for their families. Abe never became a hunter. He preferred watching animals to hunting them. One day, when he was almost eight years old, wild turkeys flocked near the Lincoln cabin. Abe was home when he heard the turkeys gobbling outside. Abe took his father's rifle, aimed it through a crack in the wall, and

25

fired. The Lincolns enjoyed a delicious turkey dinner that night! But never again would Abraham Lincoln shoot an animal. He was sad because he had killed such a beautiful bird.

One fall day in 1817, the Lincolns heard voices. In rolled Nancy's aunt and uncle, Betsy and Thomas Sparrow. With them was Abe's cousin Dennis Hanks. The newcomers moved into the Lincoln's shelter. Winter was coming and all the men, except for Abe, hunted. Abe cleared more land and chopped more wood. When spring returned, the two families planted six acres of crops.

There was no school in the Indiana wilderness yet. But Abe did not forget what he had learned before in school. He read the Bible and spelled words from the spelling book. Abe wrote letters for adults who could not write. He practiced numbers on scraps of paper. When he had no paper, Abe wrote with charcoal on a wooden shovel, erased what he had written, and practiced some more!

At night, Abe's family told Bible stories and tales about their family's history. Abe listened eagerly, hungering for new words. When he was alone, Abe shared the words and stories he learned out loud in the woods. He liked to do this so the words he learned would stay in his memory.

One day, when he was eight years old, Abe rode two miles to take a sack of grain to Mr. Gordon's flour mill. At the mill, a horse slowly turned the mill wheel to grind the grain into flour. Abe enjoyed going to the mill. He listened to farmers tell stories and jokes, and share news. Abe had gathered more stories to tell out loud when he was alone.

Night was coming. Abe was usually very patient, but the horse was going too slowly. Abe wanted to get home before dark. Abe wanted the horse to walk faster, so he hit it with a whip. The horse disagreed and kicked Abe in the forehead. Abe fell to the ground.

Someone ran to get Abe's father and Tom rushed to his son. Abe was carried home

where he lay unconscious. Finally, Abe's eyes opened. He did not say anything for a few hours, but Abe Lincoln would live!

The fall of 1818 brought the "milk sickness" to the wilderness. Pioneer families did not know what caused this feared disease that killed cows and people, and no one had a cure. Thomas and Betsy Sparrow fell ill. Nancy nursed them as best she could, but the Sparrows soon died. Tom and Dennis made two wooden coffins, and they buried Betsy and Thomas.

A few days later, Nancy Lincoln felt dizzy. She had a fever. But she did not go to bed. There was too much work to do. One night, Nancy called nine-year-old Abe and eleven-year-old Sarah to her bedside. She looked lovingly at her two children. She told them to always "be good and kind to their father, to one another, and to the world." That night, on October 5, 1818, Nancy Lincoln died.

6

ABE'S NEW MOTHER

Tom Lincoln made a coffin for Nancy from boards he cut himself. With his knife, Abe whittled pine pegs to hold the boards together. Grief-stricken, Abe, Sarah, and Dennis watched Tom bury Nancy on a wooded hill near where the deer ran. Abe was nine years old. All his life, Abe remembered his gentle mother. He called her his "angel mother."

Abe worked extra hard from dawn to dusk to ease his sadness. Sarah did the cooking and cleaning. Abe tried to cheer up his sister. Abe and Dennis caught a baby raccoon and gave the cuddly creature to Sarah. They gave her a turtle, too. They tried to catch a fawn for her. But nothing could replace Nancy Lincoln.

A year slowly passed. Dennis Hanks moved in with the Lincolns. The Lincoln home was still in mourning. Tom Lincoln knew he needed another wife to help him raise Abe and Sarah. He couldn't make a living on his farm without a partner.

Tom remembered his friend Sarah Bush in Kentucky. Sarah had married Daniel Johnston. The Johnstons had three children: Elizabeth, Matilda, and John. Then Mr. Johnston died. Sarah had no husband and three children. Tom had no wife and two children. He decided to ask Sarah Johnston to marry him. He saddled his horse and said good-bye to Abe, Sarah, and Dennis. The three would be on their own in the wilderness until Tom returned.

Sarah worked inside the cabin, Abe worked on the farm, and Dennis hunted. The days were long and lonely. One afternoon, Abe, Sarah, and Dennis heard voices. They rushed to greet the newcomers. A loaded wagon pulled by four horses rolled out of the woods. Sarah Bush Johnston Lincoln rode on

the wagon seat, a big smile on her face. With her were Abe's new stepsisters, Elizabeth and Matilda, and his new stepbrother, John. The lonely wilderness farm would not be so lonely anymore.

Abe helped unload the wagon. There were feather pillows, a kettle for making soap, and a spinning wheel. There were pots, pans, dishes, knives, forks, and spoons. There was even a walnut dresser, the first piece of furniture Abe had ever seen that had not been made by his father. And there were books!

Sarah looked at Abe, Sarah, and Dennis. Their clothes were torn and their hands, faces, and hair were dirty. Sarah decided to make them "more human." Sarah told Dennis to take a bench to the trough where the horses drank water. She told Abe and John to fill the trough with fresh water from the spring. They returned with their buckets brimming with clear water. Sarah took some soap she had made. She took the dipper, splashed Abe and Sarah, and washed them well. She combed the snarls out of Abe's and

Sarah's hair. Then she told them to dress in clean clothes.

When stepmother Sarah was finished, Dennis said Abe and Sarah looked neat and clean. Sarah worked on the cabin. No more bearskin rug for a door! She told her new husband to make a wooden door. Tom cut a window so there would be light in the cabin, then he covered the window with greased paper. No dirt floor for Sarah Bush Johnston Lincoln! She had Abe, Tom, and Dennis split logs to make a wooden floor. Next, they painted the walls and ceiling white. The new Lincoln family might live in the wilderness, but they didn't have to live like wild animals.

7

ABE GOES TO SCHOOL
BY LITTLES

Sarah made new mattresses for Abe, Dennis, and John, who slept in the loft together. Sarah was firm, but she was also gentle, kind, and had a good sense of humor. Sarah was fair, too. She had to be a mother to her own children as well as to Abe and Sarah. She made sure everyone got along well. Best of all, Sarah Bush Johnston Lincoln brought love back to the Lincoln cabin. Sarah liked Abe and Sarah, too. She knew they missed their mother, so Sarah tried to be the best mother she could be for them.

Abe grew especially fond of his stepmother. Their minds seemed to work together. Abe never said a cross word to his stepmother and he always did what she asked him to do. Abe said his stepmother "had been his best friend in the world." Sarah said Abraham Lincoln was "the best boy I ever saw or expected to see."

Stepmother Sarah wanted Abe to continue his schooling. Three months of school for a young boy was too little. Abe, Sarah, Elizabeth, and John walked a mile each way to school.

Abe's new school in Indiana was like his old Kentucky school. It was a one-room log cabin with a fireplace for heat and a window for light. Students sat on split log benches during their lessons. Abe's teacher was Andrew Crawford. The children went to Mr. Crawford's school for one term, about three months.

The next fall, they went to another school four miles away. Their teacher was Azel Dorsey. Abe had so many farm chores that he did not go to school every day. But when he could, Abe hurried through the woods to be first at school in the morning. He went bare-foot when the weather was good. In the snow, Abe wore birch-bark shoes. The soles were hickory bark. He strapped these shoes over his knitted socks. Abe concentrated on his reading, writing, and math. He practiced so he could be a good speller and he usually won the spelling bees.

Abe liked to share what he knew. One day, Abe listened as a girl tried to spell "defied" out loud. She said "D . . . e . . . f . . ." but then got stuck. Abe pointed to his eye. She got the hint and said "i." She added "e-d" and spelled the word correctly!

Once, Abe had to write an essay on a topic he felt strongly about. Abe remembered how sad he was when he shot the beautiful turkey. He wrote his essay about not harming wild animals, which was an unusual topic for a frontier boy. Pioneer boys had to be good hunters to provide food for their families, but Abe felt strongly about not hunting. He was determined to express his opinion whether or not others agreed with

him. Abe believed "that an ant's life was to it as sweet as ours to us."

Abe worked hard to have excellent penmanship. He carefully formed each letter. Once, he wrote in his copybook,

Abraham Lincoln his hand and pen
He will be good but God knows when.

Abe was a leader at school. The other students looked up to him. He was tall. He was funny and he entertained them with stories. Abe was kind and helpful. People enjoyed being around Abraham Lincoln.

Over the next few years, Abe went to three log cabin schools. He spent a little time in each one. All together, he gained nine months of schooling. His total schooling barely equaled a year. Abe liked to say he went to school "by littles" — a little school here, a little school there. When he was fifteen years old, Abe stopped going to school, even by littles.

8

ABE'S HAPPIEST DAYS

Abe loved books. He always seemed to have a book with him. Dennis Hanks said, "Abe was getting hungry for books, reading everything he could lay his hands on." Abe read the books at his schools and he was always eager to read more. Books, however, were rare on the frontier. Abe read and reread every book he could find. He memorized parts of the books. If there were words Abe especially liked, he wrote them on a board until he could find paper to write them on.

Family and friends knew Abe loved to read. They helped him find books. One friend said Abe read every book within fifty miles! Stepmother Sarah had brought books with her. Abe read her *Aesop's Fables*, *Robinson Crusoe*, and *Pilgrim's Progress*.

At night, Abe sat near the fire, tilted his chair back, and leaned his bony shoulders against the wall. He called this "sitting on his shoulder blades." When he worked in the fields, Abe put corn muffins in his pockets and tucked a book under his shirt. When he rested, Abe nibbled his muffins while reading. Abe knew books were important to understand the world stretching beyond southern Indiana, where he lived. One relative said that after working in the fields, Abe "would go to the cupboard, snatch a piece of cornbread, take down a book, sit down in a chair, cock his legs up as high as his head, and read."

One of Abe's favorite books was Mason Weem's *Life of George Washington*. George Washington became Abe's hero. When he was eighteen years old, Abe borrowed the Washington biography from a neighbor named Josiah Crawford. One night, Abe took the book to his attic loft. Later, Abe

suddenly awoke. Rain had dripped in and had ruined the book. Abe took the book to Mr. Crawford and apologized. Abe told Mr. Crawford he had no money to pay for the book, but he offered to work until he could pay him back. Mr. Crawford respected Abe for his honesty. He agreed that three days' work would equal the book's value. For the next three days, Abe worked for Mr. Crawford on his farm. He paid off his debt to Mr. Crawford and he got to keep the book!

Abe still worked for his father. Under the law, Tom Lincoln owned Abe's labor until Abe was twenty-one years old. Abe stood six feet four inches tall. He was strong from all his work on the farm. He got even stronger from chopping down trees, splitting logs into fence rails, plowing and planting the farm fields, and carrying water. Friends and neighbors admired Abe's strength. They asked Abe to help them lift logs for new cabins or barns. One day, Abe moved a six-hundred-pound chicken house. The four men who were supposed to move it stood by and watched him!

Abe felt the years in Indiana were the best of his life. He wrote he had a "joyous, happy boyhood." But Abraham Lincoln's boyhood days were over. He was twenty-one years old. Tom Lincoln had grown restless again. This time he wanted to move to Illinois. Tom sold his farm, corn, and hogs.

In March of 1830, the Lincolns loaded their household goods onto a wagon pulled by oxen. Abe prodded the oxen to keep them moving, told jokes to keep everyone's spirits up, and wondered what life in Illinois would bring his way. He helped his father establish the new family farm. Abe decided that he did not want to be a farmer all of his life, but he did not know what he wanted to be.

Abe left the farm. In 1831, at age twenty-two, he drifted into the frontier village of New Salem, Illinois. Abe got a job in the only store. At night he slept on the counter. People immediately liked Abe Lincoln. He was friendly and honest. Once he accidentally charged a woman six cents too much for tea. Abe walked six miles to return her money.

One of Abe's other jobs was to take a flatboat down the Ohio and Mississippi Rivers to New Orleans. The flatboat was loaded with live hogs, lumber, barrels, and salted meat.

When he reached New Orleans, Abe saw something he had never seen before — a slave auction. Seeing slaves bought and sold like cattle upset Abe. He said to his friend Denton Offutt, "Boy, let's get away from this. If I ever get a chance to hit that thing (slavery), I'll hit it hard."

9

ABE GETS ELECTED

In 1832, the store went out of business and Abe was out of a job. Abe had become very popular in and around New Salem. He was honest, friendly, well spoken, and had a wonderful sense of humor.

Abe had not thought about a career in politics. At the request of his friends, however, he decided to run for the legislature. As one friend said, "Lincoln had nothing, only plenty of friends." Besides, Abe could earn money working for the government.

Before the election was held, however, a war broke out between settlers and a band of Native Americans led by Chief Black Hawk. Abe joined the militia to fight. He was so popular he was elected captain. It was Abe's first election and the one he was the most proud of all his life.

Abe never fought any Native Americans. Abe said he survived "a good many bloody struggles with mosquitoes." He served three months in the militia. When Abe returned to New Salem, he stayed in the race for the Illinois legislature. He told friends, "If elected I shall be thankful; if not it will be all the same." Abe lost the election.

He went to work in another store, this time as part-owner. Abe was not a good businessman. He would rather talk with customers or read than sell things. When the store closed, Abe owed people $1,200. He promised to pay back all of the money. It took him fifteen years, but he did it!

In 1834, when he was twenty-five years old, Abe ran again for the state legislature. He won and moved to the state capital in Vandalia, Illinois. Between meetings, Abe decided to become a lawyer. He had no money to go to school, so he taught himself.

On March 1, 1837, Abraham Lincoln

passed a test and officially became a lawyer. The Illinois state capital was moved to Springfield. Abe was twenty-eight years old when he rode into Springfield on a borrowed horse. He had just seven dollars. Abe worked in the legislature for the next eight years. He also practiced law. He worked hard, won many cases, and became even more popular.

In 1840, Abe met energetic, beautiful Mary Todd at a party. Mary was visiting a cousin in Springfield. Abe enjoyed Mary's quick wit and gift of conversation. Abe was shy and wanted to dance with Mary "in the worst way."

Finally, Abe got up the courage to ask Mary to dance. After they danced, Mary agreed that Abe danced "in the worst way." Abe laughed and agreed.

Soon, Abe and Mary were taking long walks and rides together. Abe did not feel shy with Mary. He liked to talk with her and they discussed everything from horses to politics.

They did seem an unusual couple to the folks of Springfield. Abe was tall and Mary was short. Abe had grown up poor and had less than a year of school. Mary's Kentucky family was wealthy, and she was well educated and even spoke French. Abe was quiet and shy around women. Perky Mary bubbled around her many male companions.

These two opposites attracted each other and fell in love. Once, when Mary was asked whom she would marry, she said a man who would be president. On November 4, 1842, Mary and Abe were married.

Before long, Abe and Mary became the proud parents of a boy they named Robert. The Lincolns bought a house, the only house Abe ever owned. Here, the Lincolns lived for the next seventeen years. Three more Lincoln boys were born in this house: Eddie (1846), Willie (1850), and Tad (1853). Abe loved his boys. He played with them, read to them, and rarely punished them.

In 1846, at age thirty-seven, the popular Abraham Lincoln was elected to the United States House of Representatives. The Lincolns moved to Washington, D.C. Mary,

however, did not like living in Washington, so she took the boys and they moved in with her parents in Kentucky. In 1848, Abe ran again for the House. This time he lost. He met his family back in Springfield and returned to his law practice. Abe was finished with politics.

Abe's law practice often took him out of Springfield. He had to travel to meet clients and settle cases. Sometimes he rode a horse. Other times he traveled in a carriage. Abe often did not carry a case for his important papers. Instead he stuffed them in his tall black hat so he would know where they were!

Abe missed his family when he was gone. He especially missed laughing and playing with his boys. At home or at the office, Abe let his sons do whatever they wanted. They wrestled on the floor, knocked things over, and mixed up his papers. Abe had had such a hard childhood that he wanted his sons to have all the fun they could while they were young.

William Herndon, one of Abe's law partners, wrote, "If they (Abe's sons) pulled down all the books from the shelves, bent the points of all the pens, overturned the spittoon, it never disturbed the serenity of their father's good nature."

Abe, however, did enjoy the quiet time on the road when he had time to read and think. He worked hard to remember what he read. He said, "I am slow to learn and slow to forget what I have learned. My mind is like a piece of steel — very hard to scratch anything on it, and almost impossible after you get it there, to rub it out."

Abe also enjoyed meeting and making new friends while he traveled. As usual, Abe was the center of attention, telling tall tales, making jokes, and entertaining whoever he was with.

More and more folks got to know the lanky, likeable young lawyer from Springfield. If he was ever to run for office again, they told Abe they would vote for him!

On February 1, 1850, tragedy struck the Lincolns. That day, young Eddie died from tuberculosis. To ease his grief, Abe worked even harder. Sometimes he was in Springfield. Often he rode through the countryside helping people in county courts. Abe became a familiar figure around the Illinois prairie communities. He stuffed important papers in his tall hat, propped his long legs up in his carriage, opened a book, and let his horse slowly pull him to the next town.

As usual, Abe talked and told stories. He listened to what people had to say. Trouble over slavery was brewing between northern states and southern states. The problem was whether slavery would be allowed in new states that joined the United States. The Northern states said no more slavery. The Southern states wanted slavery to spread. The debate raged across the United States.

Abe agreed that no new slave state should join the Union. He knew slavery was wrong. He remembered seeing slaves chained together in Kentucky when he was five years old. Abe remembered how his family had moved from Kentucky to Indiana rather than buy slaves. He recalled how he felt when he saw slaves at a slave auction in New Orleans. He firmly believed slavery would die out in the southern states.

In 1854, Congress passed a law to let new states decide whether or not they would allow slavery. Abe had not been in politics for six years, but the new law angered him. He spoke out against the law whenever he could. By 1857, Abe was the most powerful voice in Illinois against slavery.

In 1858, forty-nine-year-old Abe ran against Stephen Douglas for a seat in the United States Senate. Douglas was for slavery. The two men debated in front of thousands of voters. Abe said, "I believe this government cannot endure permanently half-slave and half-free." Newspapers across America wrote about the Lincoln–Douglas debates. Abe won the debates, but he lost the election. Afterward he said, "I feel like the boy who stumped his toe. I am too big to cry and too badly hurt to laugh." But now, most Americans knew who Abraham Lincoln was and what he stood for.

10
PRESIDENT ABRAHAM LINCOLN

In 1860, Abe ran for president. During the election, Grace Bedell, an eleven-year-old, wrote to Abe. She suggested that he grow a beard — and he did! The Southern states did not like Lincoln. He was hated so much that his name was not even on the election ballot in the South. These states said that if Lincoln were elected, they would leave the United States.

Many people did not want Lincoln to become president. On his way to Washington, D.C., he was told people would try to kill him. At one point, Lincoln had to hide on the train so his enemies would not find him!

On March 4, 1861, Abraham Lincoln was sworn in as the sixteenth President of the

United States. He swore to uphold the laws of the country, even if it meant war with the Southern states.

Now he was President Lincoln. President Lincoln said the Southern states could not leave the Union, but they did. On April 12, 1861, in Charleston, South Carolina, Southern soldiers fired cannons on Fort Sumter. The Civil War began. The bloody war raged for four years. More American soldiers died in this war than in any other American war. This is because Americans were fighting Americans.

The war was hard on President Lincoln. He hated to see so many men and boys on both sides die in the bloody battles. He stayed up late at night trying to pick a general who could win the war. He made many trips to the telegraph office to learn the latest war news. He entertained visitors, many of whom were concerned about their sons in the war.

Still, Abe kept his sense of humor, struggling to cheer up those around him by making jokes in meetings. Abe still had time to have fun with his sons. He read to them and told them funny stories. He let them have free run of the White House. He rough-housed and wrestled with them and their friends. Once, the children pinned the President to the floor while a friend sat on his stomach!

Abe's sons had a pet turkey and two pet goats. One time the boys hitched a goat to a chair and rode it like a sled through the White House halls. Guests were upset, but President Lincoln only laughed. He let the boys build a fort on the White House roof and fire make-believe log cannons at the Rebel enemies.

During the war, the Lincolns suffered another tragedy. On February 20, 1862, their son Willie died from a fever. This was a terrible time for Abraham Lincoln. He knew how many families felt when their sons died in the war. Two of his sons, Eddie and Willie, had died, too.

On January 1, 1863, President Lincoln

signed the Emancipation Proclamation. This law freed all of the slaves in the southern states. Thousands of black men joined the Union Army. Some people tried to get President Lincoln to change his mind and not free the slaves. Lincoln responded by saying, "I am a slow walker, but I never walk backwards."

In 1864, Abraham Lincoln was elected president again. Finally, on April 9, 1865, the Southern states surrendered. The war was over! The union of all the United States still held. This had been President Lincoln's dream. But he hated the loss of life on both sides. He asked all Americans to forgive and work together to rebuild the country.

Photographs of Abraham Lincoln during the Civil War show him rapidly aging — his face wrinkled and his eyes grew sad. The war had taken its toll on Abraham Lincoln.

On April 14, 1865, Abe and Mary went to see a play, *My American Cousin*, at the Ford Theater. While they were watching the play, John Wilkes Booth, a Southerner, slipped be-

hind President Lincoln and shot him in the head. The next morning, Abraham Lincoln died. He was only fifty-six years old. One friend said, "Now he belongs to the ages."

All across America, people were sad. A train carried President Lincoln's body back to Springfield. All along the tracks, people cried and waved flags as the train rolled by.

Abraham Lincoln was buried in his beloved Springfield. Abraham Lincoln, born a poor boy in a log cabin, grew up to live in the White House. Who would have guessed Abe's future that chilly day of February 12, 1809?